ANTI-RACISM IN ACTION

Dismantling the Architecture of Racism

Timothy McGettigan, PhD
With an Introduction
by Earl Smith, PhD

Democracy Now!

You can't solve a problem with the ignorance that caused it.

- WILLIAM SHATSPEARE

CONTENTS

FOREWORD

Something has changed. Perhaps Americans have wearied of Donald Trump's racist rants, or perhaps the Covid pandemic has opened America's eyes to the existential hazards of systemic racism.

Whatever the cause, ever since George Floyd's murder there has been a sesmic shift in America's attitudes toward White Supremacy. More people from a wider range of backgrounds are speaking out against White Supremacy than at any time in the past half-century. Perhaps even longer.

Almost overnight, White Supremacy has become a dirty word. In a twinkling, Confederate statues have come down. Christopher

Columbus has been outed as a scummy reprobate. Mississippians dumped the Confederate flag, and NASCAR banned the Southern Cross at its events. All of this is encouraging, but there is much more to accomplish. The struggle must endure until White Supremacy is naught but a vague, unpleasant memory.

Forward!

TM

INTRODUCTION

Race matters in American society. Racism matters more. Anyone studying racial issues within the USA's major sociopolitical institutions (e.g., the US criminal justice system) either acknowledges this, or they deny the full implications of their data. Somehow we must find a way to terminate the

white supremacy that continues to destroy non-white Americans who are simply looking for the "life, liberty and pursuit of happiness" that is supposed to be guaranteed to ALL Americans.

In the World's Greatest Democracy racism has always been the Trump card. For most people living in the United States, race is such a fundamental concept that it is impossible for them to believe that race, as we define it in the US, is a uniquely American construct. Although other societies around the globe have hierarchies of color, none has a racial hierarchy that treats race as a political status that is transmitted intergenerationally.

Hence: Professor McGettigan's new book *Anti-Racism in Action: Dismantling the Architecture of Racism* is a timely contribution to the high stakes anti-racist activism that is taking place on the eve of the 2020 Presidential election. An election which, I sincerely hope, will oust the Racist-in-Chief from the White House.

Earl Smith, PhD

x

1 - WE CAN DO THIS!

Racism is a social construct that can be erected *and* dismantled.

1. Racist social policies create racist societies.
2. Anti-Racist policies create anti-racist societies.

2 - WHAT IS ANTI-RACISM?

Anti-racism is a type of social activism that is devoted to eradicating racism. Anti-racism is distinguishable from non-racism because anti-racism is predicated on actively taking steps to eliminate the scourge of racism. Non-racists claim to dislike racism, but are unwilling to take the necessary steps to terminate racism. Due to their passivity, non-racists help perpetuate the racist status quo.

Battling the Racist Status Quo

3 - THE USA IS "OUT TO GET" PEOPLE OF COLOR

Racism is a social construct that people erect by instituting racist social policies. Because racism is a social construct anti-racists can, in turn, dismantle racism by instituting policies that counteract it. For example, beginning in 1619, slavery became a common practice in North America. That practice continued until 1863 when President Lincoln counteracted slavery by signing the Emancipation Proclamation.

Unfortunately, White Supremacist racism is so deeply entrenched in the United States that no single act of anti-racism will be sufficient to eradicate it entirely. The Emancipation Proclamation was only designed to eradicate slavery. As a result, White Supremacist racism remained alive and well after the Civil War, and quickly coalesced into a new form of institutional racism known as Jim Crow. It took until 1964 for anti-racists to counteract Jim Crow when they secured passage of the Civil Rights Act of 1964.

The Civil Rights Parade (1964)

The Civil Rights Act put an end to Jim Crow segregation, but it did not eliminate White Supremacy.

Why?

Slavery and Segregation are two examples of White Supremacist thinking in action. By contrast, White Supremacy is a contrived mindset which convinces White Men that they are better than everyone else. Because it is a belief system, the only way to counteract White Supremacy is to annihilate the core beliefs upon which it depends.

White Supremacy has been thoroughly debunked by science, but it persists as the USA's ruling ideology because the federal government has not seen fit to denounce – and thereby discredit and counteract – the anti-scientific falsehoods upon which White Supremacy is predicated. Beginning with the Founding Fathers, the US federal government has been the primary purveyor of White

Supremacist ideology. Until the Feds formally disavow White Supremacy, white racists will cling like barnacles to their hateful beliefs:

Racist Falsehood #1: People can be separated into biologically distinguishable racial groups.

Racist Falsehood #2: So-called racial groups are biologically hierarchical (EX: Whites are "better" than Others)

The White Supremacist Ruling Ideology

If anyone doubts that White Supremacy has always been the USA's ruling ideology, please refer to Article 1, Section 2, Clause 3 of the US Constitution which contains a resounding endorsement of White Supremacy.

Representatives and direct Taxes shall be apportioned among the several States which may be included within this Union, according to their respective Numbers, which shall be determined by adding to the whole Number of free Persons, including those bound to Service for a Term of Years, and excluding Indians not taxed, three fifths of all other Persons. (Article 1, Section 2, Clause 3 of the United States Constitution)

The infamous Three-Fifths Compromise asserts that African Americans are subhuman(!) and Indigenous Peoples are worthless(!!) If you are searching for the policy foundations of White Supremacy, you need look no further.[1]

As it is currently composed, the Three-Fifths Compromise constitutes a declaration of war against indigenous peoples and persons of color. In other words, ever since the Constitution was ratified the USA has literally been "out to get" people of color. The Constitution encouraged slave traders to nab Africans and deliver them into bondage in America. The Constitution also green-lighted genocide against indigenous peoples and daylight robbery of their homelands.

Until the USA officially rescinds its Constitutional endorsement of White Supremacy, and formally ends the days of being "out to get" people of color, white racists will continue treating people of color like criminals for the capital crime of drawing breath.

No doubt some will complain that White Supremacist racism is an accidental outcome of the USA's complicated nation-building process.

Balderdash!

The USA's Founding Fathers knew precisely what they were doing when they insitutionalized White Supremacy. The Founders, with malice aforethought, instituted policies that conferred full Constitutional rights on white men, but no one else. That was not an accidental flub. The Founding Fathers instituted White Supremacist social policies because they wanted to create a White Supremacist society.

QED.

Eleanor Roosevelt and the Universal

Declaration of Human Rights

Fortunately, in 1948 the United Nations issued a Universal Declaration of Human Rights[2] which contains an exhaustive list of human rights that the Founding Fathers refused to consider. The USA has never ratified the Universal Declaration of Human Rights – primarily because doing so would spotlight every injustice that White Supremacists have perpetrated for the past 500+ years. Not surprisingly, White Supremacists have steered well clear of that democratic milestone.

So, who are White Supremacists and how did they accumulate so much power?

4 - WHITE SUPREMACIST DYSTOPIA

In addition to willful ignorance, racism is a form of sadism. Sadism is an addled frame of mind wherein people derive perverse pleasure from harming *perceived* inferiors. The idea that some people are better than others is rooted in antiquated, unscientific fallacies. Scientifically speaking, all humans are equal. Not identical, but equal. All living humans are imbued with the same genome and that is, quite literally, what makes us all equal.

Racists may insist that they are superior to the people they deplore, but racists are tragically misinformed. Racist social policies promote the deception that some people are better than others, but the biological facts speak for themselves. All humans are created equal.

The United States is supposed to be a place wherein everyone is treated equally, but the USA has never lived up to that ideal.

The Atlanta Race Massacre of 1906

The Founding Fathers utilized the principles of democracy to pillory King George III and champion a political divorce from England. But when the Founders constructed America's post-Revolutionary government, they gave lip service to democracy while deviously instituting White Supremacist social policies. For example, the Naturalization Act of 1790 made whiteness an essential precondition for US citizenship.

> ...any Alien _being a free white person,_ who shall have resided within the limits and under the jurisdiction of the United States for the term of two years, may be admitted to become a citizen (Naturalization Act of 1790).

A nation that only allows white men to become citizens is not a democracy. _It's a White Supremacist dystopia._

5 - THE ORIGINS OF WHITE SUPREMACY

Before Europeans invaded the Western Hemisphere, there was no such thing as White Supremacy. Europeans invented the fiction of White Supremacy via the Doctrine of Discovery; a rapacious social policy that contrived a pretext for robbing and murdering the indigenous inhabitants of the Western Hemisphere.

When Christopher Columbus sailed home with news that he had blundered into the Western Hemisphere, European power-brokers sensed an opportunity. On May 3, 1493, Pope Alexander VI issued a series of policy statements that have come to be known as the Doctrine of Discovery.

The Doctrine of Discovery instituted a perverse definition of Real versus 'Null' human beings that has remained the ideological basis for White Supremacist racism until this very day. White men rule, Others are subhuman.

Among other works well pleasing to the Divine Majesty and cherished of our heart, this assuredly ranks highest, that in our times especially the Catholic faith and the Christian religion be exalted and be everywhere increased and spread, that the health of souls be cared for and that <u>barbarous nations be overthrown and brought to the faith itself</u> (Papal Bull Inter Caetera, 1493).

The Doctrine of Discovery instructed European explorers to treat Christians like fellow human beings and non-Christians like non-people.

That, by the way, is how Columbus came to be known as the discoverer of America. The Western Hemisphere was home to millions of indigenous inhabitants for thousands of years prior to Columbus' arrival, but at the stroke of a pen Pope Alexander VI declared those multitudes null and void. According to the twisted logic of the Doctrine of Discovery, Columbus was the first Real Man to clap eyes on the New World and, therefore, Columbus had an exclusive right to claim ownership of it. Ever since, Europeans have treated indigenous peoples like unwelcome intruders in their own homeland.

Such is the horror of racist social policies. Once instituted, they destroy cruelly, systematically and without quarter.

6 - A GOVERNMENT OF BY AND FOR WHITE SUPREMACISTS

The Founding White Supremacists

The USA's Founding Fathers seized upon the Doctrine of Discovery's White Supremacist legacy as an alluring departure point for the World's Greatest Democracy. Every manifestation of racism is predicated on an act of dehumanization, i.e., the prejudiced misapprehension that WE are better than THEM. Convinced of their superiority, America's white male Founders instituted social policies which resonated with White Supremacist alpha-masculinity.

The fact that the US Constitution could comfortably coincide with slavery until 1863 and Jim Crow until 1964 is proof positive of the Founding Fathers' zeal for White Supremacy. The Founders wanted people of color to be on the outside looking in, and that's how the USA has operated ever since. In addition, by treating indigenous peoples as if they were worthless ("*excluding Indians not taxed*"), the Founders perpetuated the deceit that white Europeans were the New World's first and only natives.

By invalidating the humanity of indigenous peoples, white Europeans skirted blame for the monstrous crimes that they committed against innumerable Native Americans. Even though they were invaders from a foreign land, White Nativists viewed hostility from indigenous peoples as unjustified assaults upon the rightful inhabitants of American soil. Westward expansion was predicated upon merciless policies of malign neglect which inflicted genocide upon every indigenous community throughout the US. Nullifying indigenous peoples enabled White Nativists to celebrate continent-wide robbery and homicide as the virtuous project of a noble people: *Manifest Destiny!*

White Supremacy has also instigated racist social policies against many other communities of color. White Nativists have vilified LatinX communities throughout US history. The Chinese Exclusion Act of 1883 issued a racist preemptive strike against Chinese immigrants who dared aspire to the American Dream. Anti-Asian racism was also at work when President Roosevelt interned Japanese Americans during World War II. And, oh by the way, religious freedom has only grudgingly extended beyond modest variations on a predominantly Christian theme. How soon will a Muslim, or Buddhist be elected President of the USA?

White Supremacy continues to shape US policy well into the 21st century. Donald Trump is arguably the most vocally racist President in US history. He never misses an opportunity to stoke racial tensions and foment violence. Racism permeates his entire policy agenda from birtherism, to fawning over White Supremacist malefactors, calling Mexicans rapists, building the wall, banning Muslims, separating migrant families, suppressing votes, etc., etc.

Given the USA's longstanding affinity for White Supremacy, it is not surprising that an outspoken racist like Donald Trump could be elected President. Still, it is disappointing that almost two hundred and fifty years after its founding US democracy is still stuck in a quagmire of White Supremacist injustice.

That said, it is ironic indeed that the most bigoted of Presidents would preside over the greatest escalation in Civil Rights activism since the 1960s. Dismaying as Donald Trump's racism may be, there is evidence that White Supremacy is hurtling toward a precipice.

Will skin pigment racism ever become a thing of the past?

7 - ANTI-RACISM TO THE RESCUE

The Founding Fathers had, at best, a weak commitment to the principles of democracy. For the Founders, democratic ideals provided a convenient justification to sever ties with King George III. After breaking away from England, the Founders continued speaking the language of democracy while ruthlessly instituting White Supremacist policies.

In spite of the Founders' disdain for democracy, their reliance on democratic talking points created opportunities for women and people of color to fight for equality. The fact that women had to battle for over a century to obtain the right to vote speaks volumes about the Founding Fathers' disdain for democracy.

People of color had to fight even longer to win first-class citizenship. African Americans remained disenfranchised until securing passage of the Voting Rights Act of 1965. Indigenous peoples are still struggling to be recognized as full-fledged human beings.

We Must Do Better

Throughout US history women and people of color have forced the USA to become far more democratic than the Founding Fathers ever wished. Counteracting racist and sexist social policies has always been the path to building a better, brighter future for all. White Supremacy is the last and ugliest preserve of racist elitism. Doubtless the Donald Trumps of this world will cling to their dastardly privilege until the bitter end. Fortunately, the United States is a democracy wherein the Many need not cater to the whims of the Few.

It's time to drive the last nail in the coffin of White Supremacy. What type of anti-racist social policy will be required to counteract White Supremacy?

White Supremacy is rooted in the falsehood that White Guys are better than THEM (everyone else). What's needed is an anti-racist social policy which explicitly denounces White Supremacy and declares incontrovertibly that all humans are created equal. Given the venom with which White Supremacists guard their ill-gotten privilege, the odds of instituting policies that will annihilate White Privilage might seem slim. But, believe it or not, a visionary set of social policies that portend the bitter end of White Supremacy already exist: the International Bill of Human Rights.

The International Bill of Human Rights is comprised of three separate documents:

1. Universal Declaration of Human Rights
2. International Covenant on Civil and Political Rights
3. International Covenant on Economic, Social, and Cultural Rights

Astonishingly, at the urging of President Jimmy Carter, the USA ratified the International Covenant on Civil and Political Rights in 1992. The USA has not ratified the entire International Bill of Human Rights because of the dire threat that it poses for White Supremacy. But that is no longer an acceptable excuse!

We can rapidly and significantly advance the cause of terminating White Supremacy by demanding that the US ratify the two remaining elements of the International Bill of Human Rights.

It is essential for the federal government to formally express opposition to White Supremacy because, until now, the federal goverment has always implicitly and explicitly endorsed White Supremacy. Ratifying the International Bill of Human Rights won't instantaneously end racism, but it will finally put the bad guys (White Supremacists) on the outside looking in. In a post-White Supremacist America all humans -- including grumpy old white guys -- can and will be treated equally under the law. Isn't that the very least we should expect from the World's Greatest Democracy?

White Supremacy is the most damaging lie that has ever been imposed on humanity. The scope of the violence inflicted by White Supremacists beggars belief. What other rationale has em-powered greedy bastards to exterminate the denizens of entire continents?

White Supremacy will continue inflicting injury and abuse until it is denounced by every community on the planet. Ratifying the International Bill of Human Rights is an ideal next step in the pro-cesss of terminating White Supremacy. We have all the necessary tools, we need only put them to work.

We can do this!

LINKS TO OPEN SOURCE IMAGES

Cover Image - Black Lives Matter!

By Dave Meyers & Jasmine Benjamin - Anderson .Paak/ YouTube, Public Domain, https://commons.wikimedia.org/ w/index.php?curid=94220508

Image 1 - Something Has Changed

By Andrew Mercer (www.baldwhiteguy.co.nz) - Own work, CC BY-SA 4.0, https://commons.wikimedia.org/w/index.php? curid=90983435

Image 2 - Black Lives Rising

By John Lucia - https://www.flickr.com/photos/ studioseiko/27950807420/

CC BY 2.0, https://commons.wikimedia.org/w/index.php? curid=91096775

Image 3 - Attacking the Racist Satus Quo

By Adam Schiff - https://twitter.com/RepAdamSchiff/ status/1272336954571530240/photo/1 Public Do- main, https://commons.wikimedia.org/w/index.php? curid=93155578

Image 4 - George Floyd Protest

By Anonymous - The uploader on Wikimedia Commons received this from the author/copyright holder., CC0, https://commons.wikimedia.org/w/index.php?curid=91058754

Image 5 - Fight the Power

By Rhododendrites - Own work, CC BY-SA 4.0, https://commons.wikimedia.org/w/index.php?curid=91065897

Image 6 - The Emancipation Proclamation

https://commons.wikimedia.org/wiki/File:Emancipation_Proclamation.jpg

Image 7 - Civil Rights Parade (1964)

By Warren K. Leffler - https://www.loc.gov/item/2016646545/, Public Domain, https://commons.wikimedia.org/w/index.php?curid=57726589

Image 8 - White Supremacist Ruling Ideology

By Rowland Scherman - https://www.flickr.com/photos/100288576@N04/9517852232 CC BY 2.0, https://commons.wikimedia.org/w/index.php?curid=94661550

Image 9 - Slavery

By Berkley - https://www.ocf.berkeley.edu/~arihuang/academic/abg/slavery/history.html, CC BY-SA 4.0, https://commons.wikimedia.org/w/index.php?curid=92219782

Image 10 - Eleanor Roosevelt and the Universal Declaration of

Human Rights

https://upload.wikimedia.org/wikipedia/commons/3/3f/
Eleanor_Roosevelt_and_United_Nations_Universal_Declar-
ation_of_Human_Rights_in_Spanish_09-2456M_original.jpg

Image 11 - White Supremacy is Terrorism.

By Denver News - Denver Library Digital Collections, Public
Domain, https://commons.wikimedia.org/w/index.php?
curid=245973

Image 12 - The Massacre of Negroes in Atlanta (1906)

Cover of "Le Petit Journal", 7 October, 1906. Depicting the race
riots in Atlanta, Georgia. "The Lynchings in the United States:
The Massacre of Negroes in Atlanta." By Unknown author - Bib-
liothèque nationale de France, Public Domain, https://com-
mons.wikimedia.org/w/index.php?curid=78444224

Image 13 - The Columbus Myth

https://upload.wikimedia.org/wikipedia/commons/
c/c5/Columbus_-_for_gold%2C_God_and_glory_
%28IA_columbusforgoldg00dyso_0%29.pdf

Image 14 - Pope Alexander VI and the Doctrine of Disaster

By Cristofano dell'Altissimo - http://
www.comune.fe.it/diamanti/mostra_lucrezia/quadri/
q08.htm Public Domain, https://commons.wikimedia.org/w/
index.php?curid=4587671

Image 15 - The Founding White Supremacists

By Guy Moss - Own work, CC BY-SA 4.0, https://

commons.wikimedia.org/w/index.php?curid=51736291

Image 16 - Manifest Destiny

By Yam Nahar - Own work, Public Domain, https://commons.wikimedia.org/w/index.php?curid=3581682

Image 17 - The Racist in Chief

By The White House - https://www.flickr.com/photos/148748355@N05/49659517252/ Public Domain, https://commons.wikimedia.org/w/index.php?curid=88085978

Image 18 - Women's suffrage,

By LSE Library - https://www.flickr.com/photos/lselibrary/46323030125/

No restrictions, https://commons.wikimedia.org/w/index.php?curid=83213914

Image 19 - We Must Do Better

By Rowland Scherman - https://www.flickr.com/photos/100288576@N04/9517852232 CC BY 2.0, https://commons.wikimedia.org/w/index.php?curid=94661550

Image 20 - Justice for All

By Office of Joyce Beatty - https://twitter.com/RepBeatty/status/1266739763123494912

Public Domain, https://commons.wikimedia.org/w/index.php?curid=94344001

APPENDIX 1: THE UNITED NATIONS UNIVERSAL DECLARATION OF HUMAN RIGHTS

Preamble

Whereas recognition of the inherent dignity and of the equal and inalienable rights of all members of the human family is the foundation of freedom, justice and peace in the world,

Whereas disregard and contempt for human rights have resulted in barbarous acts which have outraged the conscience of mankind, and the advent of a world in which human beings shall enjoy freedom of speech and belief and freedom from fear and want has been proclaimed as the highest aspiration of the common people,

Whereas it is essential, if man is not to be compelled to have recourse, as a last resort, to rebellion against tyranny and oppression, that human rights should be protected by the rule of law,

Whereas it is essential to promote the development of friendly relations between nations,

Whereas the peoples of the United Nations have in the Charter reaffirmed their faith in fundamental human rights, in the dignity and worth of the human person and in the equal rights of men and women and have determined to promote social progress and better standards of life in larger freedom,

Whereas Member States have pledged themselves to achieve, in co-operation with the United Nations, the promotion of universal respect for and observance of human rights and fundamental freedoms,

Whereas a common understanding of these rights and freedoms is of the greatest importance for the full realization of this pledge,

Now, Therefore THE GENERAL ASSEMBLY proclaims THIS UNIVERSAL DECLARATION OF HUMAN RIGHTS as a common standard of achievement for all peoples and all nations, to the end that every individual and every organ of society, keeping this Declaration constantly in mind, shall strive by teaching and education to promote respect for these rights and freedoms and by progressive measures, national and international, to secure their universal and effective recognition and observance, both among the peoples of Member States themselves and among the peoples of territories under their jurisdiction.

Article 1.

All human beings are born free and equal in dignity and rights. They are endowed with reason and conscience and should act towards one another in a spirit of brotherhood.

Article 2.

Everyone is entitled to all the rights and freedoms set forth in this Declaration, without distinction of any kind, such as race, colour, sex, language, religion, political or other opinion, national or social origin, property, birth or other status. Furthermore, no distinction shall be made on the basis of the political, jurisdictional or international status of the country or territory to which a person belongs, whether it be independent, trust, non-self-governing or under any other limitation of sovereignty.

Article 3.

Everyone has the right to life, liberty and security of person.

Article 4.

No one shall be held in slavery or servitude; slavery and the slave trade shall be prohibited in all their forms.

Article 5.

No one shall be subjected to torture or to cruel, inhuman or degrading treatment or punishment.

Article 6.

Everyone has the right to recognition everywhere as a person before the law.

Article 7.

All are equal before the law and are entitled without any discrimination to equal protection of the law. All are entitled to equal protection against any discrimination in violation of this Declaration and against any incitement to such discrimination.

Article 8.

Everyone has the right to an effective remedy by the competent national tribunals for acts violating the fundamental rights granted him by the constitution or by law.

Article 9.

No one shall be subjected to arbitrary arrest, detention or exile.

Article 10.

Everyone is entitled in full equality to a fair and public hearing by an independent and impartial tribunal, in the determination of his rights and obligations and of any criminal charge against him.

Article 11.

(1) Everyone charged with a penal offence has the right to be presumed innocent until proved guilty according to law in a public trial at which he has had all the guarantees necessary for his defence.

(2) No one shall be held guilty of any penal offence on account of any act or omission which did not constitute a penal offence, under national or international law, at the time when it was committed. Nor shall a heavier penalty be imposed than the one that

was applicable at the time the penal offence was committed.

Article 12.

No one shall be subjected to arbitrary interference with his privacy, family, home or correspondence, nor to attacks upon his honour and reputation. Everyone has the right to the protection of the law against such interference or attacks.

Article 13.

(1) Everyone has the right to freedom of movement and residence within the borders of each state.

(2) Everyone has the right to leave any country, including his own, and to return to his country.

Article 14.

(1) Everyone has the right to seek and to enjoy in other countries asylum from persecution.

(2) This right may not be invoked in the case of prosecutions genuinely arising from non-political crimes or from acts contrary to the purposes and principles of the United Nations.

Article 15.

(1) Everyone has the right to a nationality.

(2) No one shall be arbitrarily deprived of his nationality nor denied the right to change his nationality.

Article 16.

(1) Men and women of full age, without any limitation due to race, nationality or religion, have the right to marry and to found a family. They are entitled to equal rights as to marriage, during marriage and at its dissolution.

(2) Marriage shall be entered into only with the free and full consent of the intending spouses.

(3) The family is the natural and fundamental group unit of society and is entitled to protection by society and the State.

Article 17.

(1) Everyone has the right to own property alone as well as in association with others.

(2) No one shall be arbitrarily deprived of his property.

Article 18.

Everyone has the right to freedom of thought, conscience and religion; this right includes freedom to change his religion or belief, and freedom, either alone or in community with others and in public or private, to manifest his religion or belief in teaching, practice, worship and observance.

Article 19.

Everyone has the right to freedom of opinion and expression; this right includes freedom to hold opinions without interference and to seek, receive and impart information and ideas through any media and regardless of frontiers.

Article 20.

(1) Everyone has the right to freedom of peaceful assembly and association.

(2) No one may be compelled to belong to an association.

Article 21.

(1) Everyone has the right to take part in the government of his country, directly or through freely chosen representatives.

(2) Everyone has the right of equal access to public service in his country.

(3) The will of the people shall be the basis of the authority of government; this will shall be expressed in periodic and genuine elections which shall be by universal and equal suffrage and shall be held by secret vote or by equivalent free voting procedures.

Article 22.

Everyone, as a member of society, has the right to social security and is entitled to realization, through national effort and international co-operation and in accordance with the organization and resources of each State, of the economic, social and cultural rights indispensable for his dignity and the free development of his personality.

Article 23.

(1) Everyone has the right to work, to free choice of employment, to just and favourable conditions of work and to protection against unemployment.

(2) Everyone, without any discrimination, has the right to equal pay for equal work.

(3) Everyone who works has the right to just and favourable remuneration ensuring for himself and his family an existence worthy of human dignity, and supplemented, if necessary, by other means of social protection.

(4) Everyone has the right to form and to join trade unions for the protection of his interests.

Article 24.

Everyone has the right to rest and leisure, including reasonable limitation of working hours and periodic holidays with pay.

Article 25.

(1) Everyone has the right to a standard of living adequate for the health and well-being of himself and of his family, including food, clothing, housing and medical care and necessary social services, and the right to security in the event of unemployment, sickness, disability, widowhood, old age or other lack of livelihood in circumstances beyond his control.

(2) Motherhood and childhood are entitled to special care and assistance. All children, whether born in or out of wedlock, shall enjoy the same social protection.

Article 26.

(1) Everyone has the right to education. Education shall be free, at least in the elementary and fundamental stages. Elementary education shall be compulsory. Technical and professional education shall be made generally available and higher education shall be equally accessible to all on the basis of merit.

(2) Education shall be directed to the full development of the human personality and to the strengthening of respect for human rights and fundamental freedoms. It shall promote understanding, tolerance and friendship among all nations, racial or religious groups, and shall further the activities of the United Nations for the maintenance of peace.

(3) Parents have a prior right to choose the kind of education that shall be given to their children.

Article 27.

(1) Everyone has the right freely to participate in the cultural life of the community, to enjoy the arts and to share in scientific advancement and its benefits.

(2) Everyone has the right to the protection of the moral and material interests resulting from any scientific, literary or artistic production of which he is the author.

Article 28.

Everyone is entitled to a social and international order in which the rights and freedoms set forth in this Declaration can be fully realized.

Article 29.

(1) Everyone has duties to the community in which alone the free and full development of his personality is possible.

(2) In the exercise of his rights and freedoms, everyone shall be subject only to such limitations as are determined by law solely for the purpose of securing due recognition and respect for the

rights and freedoms of others and of meeting the just requirements of morality, public order and the general welfare in a democratic society.

(3) These rights and freedoms may in no case be exercised contrary to the purposes and principles of the United Nations.

Article 30.

Nothing in this Declaration may be interpreted as implying for any State, group or person any right to engage in any activity or to perform any act aimed at the destruction of any of the rights and freedoms set forth herein.

---

[1] This is also why activists insist that Black Lives Matter. The Three-Fifths Compromise asserts the opposite.
[2] See Appendix 1

ABOUT THE AUTHOR

Timothy Mcgettigan

Tim McGettigan is a professor of sociology at Colorado State University - Pueblo. McGettigan and his colleague, Prof. Earl Smith, are sincerely hoping to bid farewell to White Supremacy in their lifetimes.

BOOKS BY THIS AUTHOR

A Formula For Eradicating Racism: Debunking White Supremacy

In this book, Tim McGettigan and Earl Smith make the unprecedented argument that racism is a remediable form of suggestion-induced sadism. The authors explain in plain terms how societies like the USA construct racism, and put forward a practical plan to eradicate racism in the USA and all over the world.

The Politics Of Marijuana: A New Paradigm

The phenomenon of "legal cannabis" is instigating a great deal of new research, political intrigue, and social change. The Politics of Marijuana: A New Paradigm explores the socio-political dimensions of cannabis as the world transitions from Harry Anslinger's Reefer Madness prohibition to an as-yet-to-be-defined future. This book brings together a wide variety of perspectives on the past, present, and fast-changing future of cannabis.

Captain Quark And The Time Cheaters : Donald Trump's Favorite Sci-Fi Novel -- Not!!

Universes are colliding. Characters from a tangle of universes—Star Trek, Marvel Comics, Star Wars, Harry Potter, DC Comics, Middle Earth and more—are colliding in a reality that has gone mad.

The evil, orange-skinned usurper, Uranus Blowhard, has hypnotized Amerricans with this mind-numbing MAGA chant. Blowhard is determined to collect the five Time Cheaters that will make him the most powerful roach motel tycoon in the Infiniverse. The only thing standing in Blowhard's way is Captain Quark and his crack team of superheroes, The Funtastic Five.

Will Quark and the FF thwart Blowhard's scheme to conquer the Infiniverse? The only place to find out is in the brain-tingling pages of CAPTAIN QUARK AND THE TIME CHEATERS!!

Read on MacDuff!